## OUR GREAT STATES

# WHAT'S GREAT ABOUT
# NEW HAMPSHIRE?

Peachtree

✳ Rebecca Rissman

LERNER PUBLICATIONS ✳ MINNEAPOLIS

# CONTENTS

Copyright © 2015
by Lerner Publishing Group, Inc.

Content Consultant: John Lund, PhD, Professor of History, Keene State College

Special thanks to Jack and Hunter Lund

Lerner Publications Company
A division of Lerner Publishing Group, Inc.
241 First Avenue North
Minneapolis, MN 55401 USA

For reading levels and more information, look up this title at www.lernerbooks.com.

Main body text set in ITC Franklin Gothic Std Book Condensed 12/15.
Typeface provided by Adobe Systems.

Library of Congress Cataloging-in-Publication Data

Rissman, Rebecca.
    What's great about New Hampshire? / by Rebecca Rissman.
        pages    cm. — (Our great states)
    Includes index.
    Audience: Ages 7–11.
    ISBN 978-1-4677-3858-3 (lib. bdg. : alk. paper) — ISBN 978-1-4677-6082-9 (pbk.) — 978-1-4677-6260-1 (EB pdf)
    1.  New Hampshire—Juvenile literature. I. Title.
F34.3.R57 2015
974.2–dc23                        2014029145

Manufactured in the United States of America
1 – PC – 12/31/14

# NEW HAMPSHIRE Welcomes You!

New Hampshire is a great place to visit. It has snowy mountains, historic museums, and sunny beaches. Can you smell the popcorn and the fresh cotton candy? Spend a day exploring Canobie Lake Park. Thrill seekers will love checking out Gunstock Mountain Resort. Or maybe you'd like to spend the day at Hampton Beach. Whatever you're in the mood for, New Hampshire has it. Keep reading to learn about ten things to do in this great state!

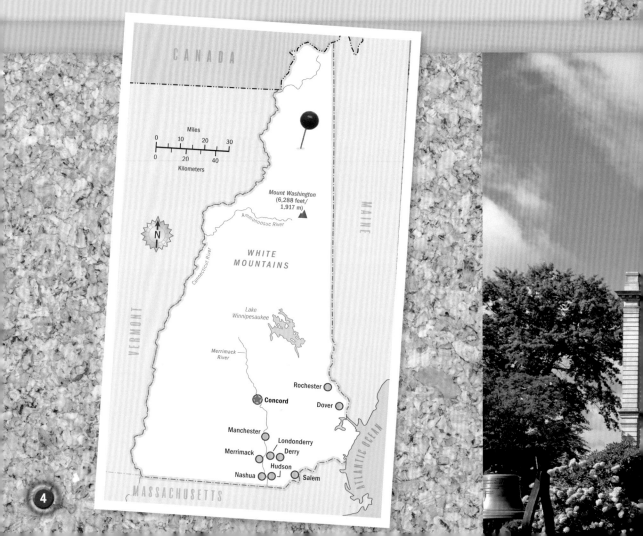

CANADA

Miles
0    10    20    30
0       20       40
Kilometers

Mount Washington
(6,288 feet/
1,917 m)

Ammonoosuc River

N

WHITE
MOUNTAINS

Connecticut River

VERMONT

MAINE

Lake
Winnipesaukee

Merrimack
River

Rochester

Concord

Dover

Manchester

Londonderry

Merrimack          Derry

Hudson

Nashua          Salem

ATLANTIC OCEAN

MASSACHUSETTS

Explore New Hampshire's parks and all the places in between! Just turn the page to find out about the GRANITE STATE. >

# GUNSTOCK MOUNTAIN RESORT

> Picture yourself speeding down a snowy mountain trail. You grip the handles of a brightly colored snow tube. Each tiny bump on the 1,068-foot (326-meter) snowy trail sends you bouncing. You can enjoy this trail and fifty-four other ski and snowboard slopes at Gunstock Mountain Resort in Gilford.

If you don't feel the need for speed, check out some of the park's thirty-two cross-country skiing trails. Strap on a pair of cross-country skis or snowshoes. Then take in the beautiful views of Gunstock Mountain while you work up a sweat.

There are fun activities to enjoy during the summer months too. Sign up for the ZipTour zip lines. Zip across more than 1.6 miles (2.6 kilometers) of zip lines on this two-hour adventure. You'll get great views of the ski trails as you fly above the trees. After the zip lines, check out the Aerial Treetop Adventures. Workers will help you into a safety harness. Then they will teach you how to climb across rope ladders, bridges, and swings that are high up in the trees!

**Try snowshoeing (*left*) or zip-lining (*right*) on your trip to Gunstock Mountain Resort.**

# POORE FAMILY HOMESTEAD HISTORIC FARM MUSEUM

> Step back in time to the mid-1800s when you visit the Poore Family Homestead Historic Farm Museum. This 100-acre (40-hectare) historic farm is in Stewartstown. Here you can experience what life was like for settlers in New Hampshire.

Walk through the museum first. You'll see clothing, newspapers, magazines, and letters dating back to the Civil War (1861–1865). The museum also has historic tools and covered wagons on display.

After exploring the museum, watch one of the farm's Mountain Men demonstrations. These outdoorsmen will show you how New Hampshire trappers survived in the wilderness. They can teach you how to build a fire. End your visit with a picnic or a trail hike on the farm's nature trails.

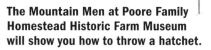

The Mountain Men at Poore Family Homestead Historic Farm Museum will show you how to throw a hatchet.

# SQUAM LAKES NATURAL SCIENCE CENTER

> Did you hear a howl? It sounds like a coyote—and it's close! If you're brave enough, explore Squam Lakes Natural Science Center in Holderness. Here you can spot mountain lions, black bears, bobcats, and coyotes in their natural habitat. Don't worry! The animals are all safely enclosed. How many different animals do you see?

After you've seen all the animals, take a hike. Climb the 1-mile (1.6-km) Mount Fayal Trail. You'll be able to see Squam Lake. At the top of the trail, you can also see Piper Homestead. You'll see parts of the farmhouse and the barn.

After your hike, relax on a Squam Lake cruise. These ninety-minute boat rides are guided tours of the lake. Can you catch a glimpse of a bald eagle or a loon through your binoculars?

Moose are among the wild animals you may see at the Squam Lakes Natural Science Center.

## SAVING THE LOON

Loons live on Squam Lake. But this bird species is in danger. New buildings and other human-made projects have affected the loon population. These projects have taken over space the birds call home. Pollution from chemicals has also been bad for the birds. These problems make it hard for loons to live in New Hampshire. Special groups have formed to protect the loon and its habitat.

# CANOBIE LAKE PARK

> Test your adventurous side with a day at Canobie Lake Park in Salem. Here you can enjoy exciting rides and delicious treats. At night, take in some live entertainment. When you arrive at the park, you'll smell sweet cotton candy. Listen for the *click*, *click*, *click* of the roller coasters.

If you're not afraid of heights, try the Corkscrew roller coaster. Or if you like spinning, try Wipeout. This ride will make you dizzy. Take a ride in an antique car or on the Canobie Express steam train. If you're looking to cool off on a hot day, check out the Tall Timber Splash waterslide. Sit in a rubber raft as you speed through twists and turns.

All that laughing and screaming is sure to make you tired. Sit back and enjoy a live show. Watch a magician pull a bird out of a hat. Or sing along with an impersonator of the pop star Michael Jackson. Before you know it, you'll be ready for more rides!

Choose your favorite animal to ride on Canobie Lake Park's merry-go-round.

Be sure to pick up a classic treat such as a funnel cake.

# MCAULIFFE-SHEPARD DISCOVERY CENTER

> Launch into orbit at the McAuliffe-Shepard Discovery Center in Concord. Learn more about space shuttles, astronauts, and working in space. The Living and Working in Space exhibit has a collection of real astronaut tools. Be sure to check out the model of a space shuttle. A video gives you more information about each part of the shuttle. Take a minute to look at the satellite images showing Earth from space.

The museum also has a satellite radio that uses Morse code. During some parts of the year, you can use the radio to say hello to the astronauts working on the International Space Station. Volunteer radio operators help you tap out a message. Maybe you'll be lucky and get a response!

Practice being a weather forecaster in another exhibit. You'll get to use high-tech equipment. End your visit by stopping at the planetarium theater. A video system lets you see more than 110,000 stars on the ceiling.

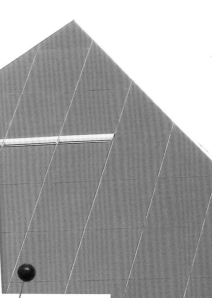

Pretend you're driving a space shuttle at the McAuliffe-Shepard Discovery Center.

See a piece of moon rock that astronauts carried back from a trip to the moon in 1972. It is on display at the Discovery Center.

# RUGGLES MINE

> Pack your hammer and a bucket—it's time to hunt for sparkling treasures at Ruggles Mine. This two-hundred-year-old mine in Grafton is a great place for explorers and treasure hunters. Ruggles Mine is mostly an open pit, but it also has many rooms and tunnels to explore.

The walls of the Ruggles Mine canyon are filled with sparkling quartz. Use a hammer to break off a piece. You can take the minerals you collect home with you! Keep searching. There are more than 150 minerals to find at the mine.

Once you've collected minerals, put on a headlamp and go exploring! Search the caves, the arches, and the tunnels. Some of the rock formations are natural. Miners created other rock formations. See if you can tell the difference.

You'll see many different colored minerals as you explore Ruggles Mine.

## MINING

Mining for rocks and minerals is an important part of New Hampshire's economy. There are many granite quarries in the state. These sites helped New Hampshire earn its nickname: the Granite State.

# FUNSPOT

> New Hampshire may be a small state, but it is home to the largest arcade in the world. Make a visit to Funspot in Laconia part of your journey through New Hampshire. There are more than six hundred games to try, including three hundred classic arcade games.

Get behind the wheel of a turbocharged race car. Then go shooting for ducks. Fight aliens and dance for your life! Whatever video game you can think of, you'll find it at Funspot. Don't forget to play *Hercules*, the biggest pinball game in the world.

Be sure to trade in your arcade tickets for prizes. Then head to the twenty-lane bowling center. Throw a few strikes and cheer on your friends. Or you can enjoy a game of miniature golf. Funspot has two different courses to choose from. And if you're visiting at night, be sure to sign up for bingo. You may win big!

Enjoy a game of bingo (*left*) or Skee-Ball (*right*) during your visit to Funspot.

# WHITE MOUNTAINS

> Eastern New Hampshire is home to the White Mountain range. These rugged peaks are great places to explore. If you're not afraid of heights, check out Mount Washington. This is the highest mountain peak in New England. It reaches 6,288 feet (1,917 m) high.

Hop on the Cog Railway, a historic steam engine train. Enjoy your ride to the top of Mount Washington. Many riders have to look away from the large windows because the steep cliff views can be scary!

If you'd rather not travel by train, try dogsledding during the winter. At Mount Washington Resort, sign up for a ride along the Ammonoosuc River. Enjoy the twists, the turns, the hills, and the sights. And when you're done, don't forget to thank your pullers with a little scratch behind the ears. You can also travel by car along the White Mountain Trail scenic drive. Maybe you'll stop at some waterfalls along the road!

## WHITE MOUNTAINS

The White Mountains cover nearly one-fourth of New Hampshire. There are forty-eight peaks in this beautiful mountain range. Many are more than 4,000 feet (1,219 m) high. The mountains are part of the White Mountain National Forest. This forest stretches across 800,000 acres (323,749 hectares) of New Hampshire.

Enjoy views of three states and the Atlantic Ocean when the Cog Railway takes you to the top of Mount Washington.

# HAMPTON BEACH

> With all of New Hampshire's inland activities, it can be easy to forget about its amazing ocean access. Tourists from around the world enjoy spending time on the state's beautiful beaches.

You can visit the beach too. Make your way to Hampton Beach in Hampton. Take off your shoes and feel the warm sand between your toes. Enjoy a chilly dip in the Atlantic Ocean. Then wrap up in a fluffy towel while you look for seashells.

After your seashell hunt, walk the 1-mile-long (1.6 km) boardwalk. Sample some freshly fried onion rings. If you're still hungry, try some of the freshest seafood in the world at one of the local restaurants. Yum!

Then make your way to the Seashell stage. Hampton is known for its nightly live music shows. Listen and dance along with the music. Some nights there are fireworks after the music. Watch the different shapes pop and boom in the sky. Remember to pack a sweater. The beach can get chilly at night!

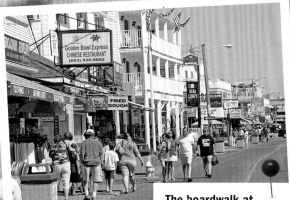

The boardwalk at Hampton Beach is full of delicious foods to try.

## NEW HAMPSHIRE'S ECONOMY

In the past, much of New Hampshire's economy relied on fishing and shipping by sea. The Atlantic Ocean helped boost the state's economy. These industries are less important for the state today. Technology industries are more important. However, many people still visit New Hampshire to fish for fun.

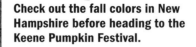
Check out the fall colors in New Hampshire before heading to the Keene Pumpkin Festival.

# JACK-O'-LANTERNS GALORE

> New England's fall colors are famous around the world. Tourists rush to New Hampshire during the fall. They hope to see the beautiful orange, red, and yellow leaves. They might enjoy a cup of hot apple cider too.

After seeing the fall leaves, take a trip to the Keene Pumpkin Festival. Each year, the citizens of Keene try to light enough jack-o'-lanterns to set a Guinness World Record. There were more than thirty thousand pumpkins on display in 2013. They set a record that year.

Be sure to see the famous tower of pumpkins at the festival. The wooden structure holds thousands of flickering pumpkins. Find your favorite face in the bunch. Then try a pumpkin-flavored snack or other fair foods. A fun activity is pumpkin bowling. Try knocking down as many pins as you can with a pumpkin.

**Bring your own carved pumpkin to add to the pumpkin display!**

## YOUR TOP TEN!

You have read about ten amazing things to see and do in New Hampshire. Now, think about what your New Hampshire top ten list would include. What would you like to see if you were to visit the state? Would you want to hike, go skiing, or lie on the beach? What activities are most exciting to you? What would you tell your friends to do if they visited New Hampshire? Keep these things in mind as you make your own top ten list.

# NEW HAMPSHIRE BY MAP

## > MAP KEY

⬟ Capital city

◯ City

◯ Point of interest

▲ Highest elevation

–··– International border

–·– State border

Visit www.lerneresource.com to learn more about the state flag of New Hampshire.

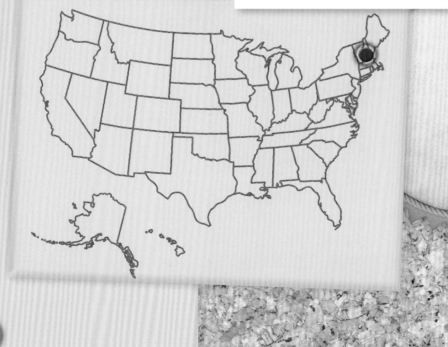

CANADA

Poore Family
Homestead Historic
Farm Museum
(Stewartstown)

Miles
0   10   20   30
0      20      40
Kilometers

Mount Washington
(6,288 feet/
1,917 m)

Ammonoosuc River

N

WHITE
MOUNTAINS

Connecticut River

VERMONT

MAINE

Squam Lakes
Natural Science Center
(Holderness)

Lake
Winnipesaukee

Gunstock
Mountain Resort
(Gilford)

Ruggles Mine
(Grafton)

Funspot
(Laconia)

Rochester

Dover

McAuliffe-Shepard
Discovery Center

Concord

Merrimack
River

Hampton
Beach
(Hampton)

Manchester

Londonderry
Derry

Merrimack

Hudson

Salem

Keene Pumpkin
Festival
(Keene)

Nashua

Canobie Lake Park

MASSACHUSETTS

ATLANTIC OCEAN

27

# NEW HAMPSHIRE FACTS

**NICKNAME:** The Granite State

**SONG:** "Old New Hampshire" by John F. Holmes

**MOTTO:** "Live Free or Die"

> **FLOWER:** common lilac

**TREE:** white birch

> **BIRD:** purple finch

**ANIMAL:** white-tailed deer

**DATE AND RANK OF STATEHOOD:** June 21, 1788; the 9th state

**CAPITAL:** Concord

**AREA:** 9,280 square miles (24,035 sq. km)

**AVERAGE JANUARY TEMPERATURE:** 19°F (–7°C)

**AVERAGE JULY TEMPERATURE:** 68°F (20°C)

**POPULATION AND RANK:** 1,323,459; 42nd (2013)

**MAJOR CITIES AND POPULATIONS:** Manchester (110,378), Nashua (87,137), Concord (42,419), Derry (33,008), Dover (30,510)

**NUMBER OF US CONGRESS MEMBERS:** 2 representatives, 2 senators

**NUMBER OF ELECTORAL VOTES:** 4

> **NATURAL RESOURCES:** lumber, mining

> **AGRICULTURAL PRODUCTS:** apples, beef cattle, hay, maple products, milk

**MANUFACTURED GOODS:** computer and electronic products, machinery

# GLOSSARY

**canyon:** a deep gorge that usually has a river or stream flowing through it

**habitat:** the natural home of a living thing

**homestead:** a house, farm, and related outbuildings

**impersonator:** a person who pretends to be another person

**Morse code:** a system of sending messages that uses long and short sounds, flashes of light, or marks to represent letters and numbers

**quarry:** an open area where people find stone, slate, or minerals

**quartz:** a type of mineral that is often shiny or sparkly

**settler:** a person who goes to live in a new place where usually there are few people

**trapper:** a person who uses a device to catch animals

LERNER
**e**
SOURCE™

Expand learning beyond the printed book. Download free, complementary educational resources for this book from our website, www.lerneresource.com.

# FURTHER INFORMATION

**America's Library**
http://www.americaslibrary.gov/es/index.php
Explore New Hampshire at America's library. Learn about the colony and its history. Then click on another state to keep learning!

Cunningham, Kevin. *The New Hampshire Colony.* New York: Scholastic, 2011. Read this book to learn about what life was like for people in colonial New Hampshire.

**50States: New Hampshire**
http://www.50states.com/newhamps.htm#VCmRPrEo6Uk
This website is a great resource for quick facts about New Hampshire and the rest of the fifty states.

**New Hampshire Fish and Game**
http://www.wildlife.state.nh.us/Wildlife/wildlife_profiles.htm
Go to this website to learn about some of the wild animals you can see in New Hampshire. Make sure to download a guide to New Hampshire animal tracks and footprints while you're there!

Shannon, Terry Miller. *From Sea to Shining Sea: New Hampshire.* New York: Children's Press, 2009. This kid-friendly book provides a simple introduction to the people, the history, the geography, the plants, and the animals of New Hampshire.

# INDEX

## PHOTO ACKNOWLEDGMENTS

The images in this book are used with the permission of: © Michael Shake/Shutterstock Images, p. 1; NASA, pp. 2–3; © Laura Westlund/Independent Picture Service, pp. 4, 27; © Olivier Le Queinec/Shutterstock Images, pp. 4–5; © Boudewijn Sluijk/Shutterstock Images, p. 5; © Jim Cole/AP/Corbis, pp. 6–7; © My Good Images/Shutterstock Images, p. 7 (left); © Alxcrs/Shutterstock Images, p. 7 (right); © Jerry & Marcy Monkman/Danita Delimont Photography/Newscom, pp. 8–9; © Tim Pleasant/Shutterstock Images, p. 9; Abigail Batchelder, pp. 10–11; Public Domain, pp. 11 (top), 12–13; © Michelle Lalancette/Shutterstock Images, p. 11 (bottom); © Thinkstock, p. 13 (top); © Brent Hofacker/Shutterstock Images, p. 13 (bottom); © David R. Frazier Photolibrary, Inc./Alamy, pp. 14–15; © David R. Frazier/Danita Delimont Photography/Newscom, p. 15 (top); Timothy Taber, p. 15 (bottom); James Walsh, pp. 16–17; Mike Fisher, p. 17 (top); Library of Congress, pp. 17 (bottom) (LC-D4-36225), 23 (bottom) (LC-D4-70415); Rob Boudon, pp. 18–19, 19 (right); © Melanie Braun/Shutterstock Images, p. 19 (left); © Anton Oparin/Shutterstock Images, p. 20; © Jeffrey M. Frank/Shutterstock Images, pp. 20–21; © Richard Cavalleri/Shutterstock Images, p. 21; © Alan Briere/DK Images, pp. 22–23; © Kevin Galvin/Newscom, p. 23 (top); © Sean Patrick Doran/Shutterstock Images, p. 24; © Michael Springer/Zuma Press/Newscom, pp. 24–25; © Denis Vrublevski/Shutterstock Images, p. 25; © nicoolay/iStockphoto, p. 26; © torikell/Shutterstock Images, p. 29 (top right); © Steve Byland/Shutterstock Images, p. 29 (top left); © Kletr/Shutterstock Images, p. 29 (bottom right); © Alexander Chaikin/Shutterstock Images, p. 29 (bottom left).

Cover: © age fotostock/SuperStock (railway); © Jose Azel/Getty Images (hiker); © Rod Chronister/Dreamstime.com (pumpkins); © Laura Westlund/Independent Picture Service (map); © iStockphoto.com/fpm (seal); © iStockphoto.com/vicm (pushpins); © iStockphoto.com/benz190 (corkboard).